Dates: _____ to _____

Name: _____

Courses: _____

_____

The Golf Stats Log Book

Record detailed statistics for 40 rounds of golf

Chris McMullen

The Golf Stats Log Book

Copyright (c) 2008 Chris McMullen

All rights reserved. This includes the right to reproduce any portion of this book in any form.

Custom Books

Nonfiction / sports / golf

ISBN: 1438279639

EAN-13: 9781438279633

Using this log book

After completion of each round of golf, enter detailed statistics in this record book.

The comprehensive statistics of this log book are organized to help you identify which aspects of your game you need to work on most to help you shoot lower scores, including short irons and wedges, mid- and long irons, fairway woods, driving, pitching, chipping, sand saves, putting, and mental toughness.

After every 10 rounds, compile your 10-round average and compare with prior 10-round averages to see which skills are improving or getting worse.

Study your statistics in the various categories to help decide what to practice or take lessons on.

If you have a sharp memory, you may be able to complete each round's log when you return from the golf course. Otherwise, you should make notes on your scorecard to help you complete the logs. For example, in addition to recording your score, you can record how many putts you had on each hole, whether you hit a GIR or a fairway, how close you were to the hole, how close you lagged a putt to the hole, etc. Review the stats in this log book to see what notes you may need to record on your scorecard that you may otherwise not remember.

Following are some explanations to help you enter your statistics:

Scoring: Gross is your unadjusted score; net is what you obtain after subtracting your handicap from your gross score. For example, if you have a 14 handicap and shoot 88, your gross score is 88 and your net score is 74.

If you have a handicap of 18 or higher, consider recording eagles, birdies, pars, bogeys, and others based on your net score for each hole rather than your gross score.

For par 3's, par 4's, and par 5's, enter your score relative to par (or if you prefer, relative to your handicapped par). For example, if there are four par 3's and your scores are 4, 5, 2, and 4, enter +3 for par 3 performance.

Greens in Regulation: Enter the number of greens hit and break it down by short irons and wedges, mid- and long irons, and fairway woods or hybrids. Base greens hit on your driving distance rather than par. For example, if you drive the ball 200 yards, you should reach a 370-yard hole in two strokes and a 430-yard hole in three strokes. So, if you reach a 430-yard hole in three strokes, it counts as a green in regulation relative to your length, but if you reach a 370-yard hole in three strokes it does not count as a green in regulation.

The slash (/) indicates that you should enter a fraction. For example, if you attempted to reach 6 greens in regulation with a wood and came through 2 times, record this as 2 / 6.

Greens Under Regulation: If you reach a green that you can barely reach with all your effort, or if you have an eagle putt, count this as a green under regulation. Compare your attempts to your successes and also separate par 4 and par 5 performance.

Shot-making: This category will help you assess how well you are hitting your wedges, short irons, mid-irons, and long irons.

Control: This category will help you compare how many times you miss greens to the left compared to the right. If you miss most of the greens to the left, for example, you either need to work on this on the range or compensate for it on the course.

Short Iron and Wedge Performance: Record how close you hit your short irons and wedges to the pin, and how many greens you miss with these clubs. Knocking these clubs close is an important key to better scoring.

Fairways Hit: Record how many fairways you hit, and also break this down by club.

Driving: Keep track of what types of drives you hit – both the quality of the shot and the direction. A <u>push</u> goes straight to the right, whereas a <u>slice</u> curves to the right; a <u>pull</u> goes straight left, and a <u>hook</u> curves to the left. Count fades and draws that end up on target as straight shots: A fade starts left and curves back to the fairway, while a draw starts right and curves left to the target. Any drive that is significantly shorter than average because it was hit fat or off-center should be counted as short.

Putting: Break down your putting performance. Under GIR, total the number of putts hit on greens in regulation. For putts per GIR, divide the number of GIR putts by the number of greens in regulation hit. For example, if you hit 12 greens in regulation and have 18 putts on those 12 holes, your putts per GIR is 18 divided by 12, which is 1.50.

One Putts: Keep track of how many one-putts you make, separated by distance and what you were shooting for. If you make a lot of par putts from 10', but miss a lot of birdie putts from this same distance, for example, then you can see that you need to work on how to handle the pressure of putting for a birdie.

Missed Putts: Here you can assess whether you miss more putts left or right, as well as short or long. Count a putt as long if it went more than two feet past the hole, since the ideal distance of a putt is 18 inches past.

Lag Putts: For long putts, record how many are lagged close or far to rate how good your lag putting is.

Chipping: Keep track of chip-ins and how well you hit your chips.

Pitching: Here, you can assess how well you are pitching and, if you need improvement in this area, what you need to work on.

Sand Play: The conventional sand saves stat in itself can be misleading: It doesn't tell you whether your bunker play or putting need work, or both. These detailed sand play stats will help you assess this clearly. Miss means missed the green, and left in is a shot that didn't leave the trap.

Mental Toughness: The mental aspect of the game has a significant effect on scoring. Bounce back is how often you do well on a hole following a bad hole. If you're a pro, you worry about how many times you make birdie right after you make a bogey or worse. Otherwise, work with net bogeys and net birdies.

Record how many good and poor decisions you make. If you have mostly good decisions, it should give you confidence in your decision-making in the future. If you made many poor decisions, you should realize that you need to make plans before your round and stick with them during the round.

Keep track of risks – like trying to hit a fairway wood over water or laying up short with an iron. Keep track of how often the risk pays off or doesn't, and how often laying up pays off or doesn't. This stat can help you make better decisions in the future.

Lapses in concentration and swings made when angry or rushed can lower your score, so these are worth recording.

Penalties: Keep track of how many strokes are lost to penalties, and whether they are out of bounds (OB), lost balls, or water balls.

Course				Yardage		Date	
			Scoring				
gross		front 9		back 9		net	
eagles		birdies		pars		bogeys	
others		par 3's		par 4's		par 5's	
			Greens in Regulation				
total	/ 18	7I - SW	/	1I - 6I	/	woods	/
			Greens Under Regulation				
attempts		success		par 4's	/	par 5's	/
			Shot-making				
wedges		short irons		mid-irons		long irons	
quality		quality		quality		quality	
fair		fair		fair		fair	
poor		poor		poor		poor	
			Control				
wedges		short irons		mid-irons		long irons	
straight		straight		straight		straight	
left		left		left		left	
right		right		right		right	
			Short Irons / Wedges Hit to Within:				
0' - 10'		10' - 30'		30' +		missed	
			Fairways Hit				
total	/	driver	/	3W - 5W	/	irons	/
			Driving				
quality		straight		solid		short	
fair		left		pulled		hooked	
poor		right		pushed		sliced	

The Golf Stats Log Book

Putting						
total		front 9		back 9		GIR	
1 putts		2 putts		3 putts		per GIR	
One Putts						
inside 5'	/	5' - 10'	/	10' - 20'	/	20' +	/
birdies	/	pars	/	bogeys	/	other	/
Missed Putts						
right		left		short		2' + long	
Long Putts Lagged to Within:						
tap-in		1' - 3'		3' - 5'		5' +	
Chipping						
holed		quality		fair		poor	
Pitching						
holed		quality		fair		poor	
chilly dip		pinched		skulled		fluffed	
Sand Play						
saves		0' - 5'		5' - 10'		10' +	
missed		left in		fat		skulled	
Mental Toughness						
bounce back	/	risks rewarded	/	lapses	
good decisions		risks punished	/	angry swings	
poor decisions		risks safely avoided	/	rushed swings	
Penalties						
total		OB		lost		water	

Course				Yardage		Date	
\multicolumn{8}{c}{Scoring}								
gross		front 9		back 9		net	
eagles		birdies		pars		bogeys	
others		par 3's		par 4's		par 5's	
\multicolumn{8}{c}{Greens in Regulation}								
total	/ 18	7I - SW	/	1I - 6I	/	woods	/
\multicolumn{8}{c}{Greens Under Regulation}								
attempts		success		par 4's	/	par 5's	/
\multicolumn{8}{c}{Shot-making}								
wedges		short irons		mid-irons		long irons	
quality		quality		quality		quality	
fair		fair		fair		fair	
poor		poor		poor		poor	
\multicolumn{8}{c}{Control}								
wedges		short irons		mid-irons		long irons	
straight		straight		straight		straight	
left		left		left		left	
right		right		right		right	
\multicolumn{8}{c}{Short Irons / Wedges Hit to Within:}								
0' - 10'		10' - 30'		30' +		missed	
\multicolumn{8}{c}{Fairways Hit}								
total	/	driver	/	3W - 5W	/	irons	/
\multicolumn{8}{c}{Driving}								
quality		straight		solid		short	
fair		left		pulled		hooked	
poor		right		pushed		sliced	

Putting								
total		front 9		back 9		GIR	
1 putts		2 putts		3 putts		per GIR	
One Putts								
inside 5'		/	5' - 10'	/	10' - 20'	/	20' +	/
birdies		/	pars	/	bogeys	/	other	/
Missed Putts								
right		left		short		2' + long	
Long Putts Lagged to Within:								
tap-in		1' - 3'		3' - 5'		5' +	
Chipping								
holed		quality		fair		poor	
Pitching								
holed		quality		fair		poor	
chilly dip		pinched		skulled		fluffed	
Sand Play								
saves		0' - 5'		5' - 10'		10' +	
missed		left in		fat		skulled	
Mental Toughness								
bounce back		/	risks rewarded	/		lapses	
good decisions			risks punished	/		angry swings	
poor decisions			risks safely avoided	/		rushed swings	
Penalties								
total		OB		lost		water	

Course				Yardage		Date	
\multicolumn{8}{c}{Scoring}							

Course				Yardage		Date	
gross		front 9		back 9		net	
eagles		birdies		pars		bogeys	
others		par 3's		par 4's		par 5's	
Greens in Regulation							
total	/ 18	7I - SW	/	1I - 6I	/	woods	/
Greens Under Regulation							
attempts		success		par 4's	/	par 5's	/
Shot-making							
wedges		short irons		mid-irons		long irons	
quality		quality		quality		quality	
fair		fair		fair		fair	
poor		poor		poor		poor	
Control							
wedges		short irons		mid-irons		long irons	
straight		straight		straight		straight	
left		left		left		left	
right		right		right		right	
Short Irons / Wedges Hit to Within:							
0' - 10'		10' - 30'		30' +		missed	
Fairways Hit							
total	/	driver	/	3W - 5W	/	irons	/
Driving							
quality		straight		solid		short	
fair		left		pulled		hooked	
poor		right		pushed		sliced	

\multicolumn{9}{c}{Putting}
total		front 9		back 9		GIR	
1 putts		2 putts		3 putts		per GIR	
\multicolumn{9}{c}{One Putts}
inside 5'	/	5' - 10'	/	10' - 20'	/	20' +	/
birdies	/	pars	/	bogeys	/	other	/
\multicolumn{9}{c}{Missed Putts}
right		left		short		2' + long	
\multicolumn{9}{c}{Long Putts Lagged to Within:}
tap-in		1' - 3'		3' - 5'		5' +	
\multicolumn{9}{c}{Chipping}
holed		quality		fair		poor	
\multicolumn{9}{c}{Pitching}
holed		quality		fair		poor	
chilly dip		pinched		skulled		fluffed	
\multicolumn{9}{c}{Sand Play}
saves		0' - 5'		5' - 10'		10' +	
missed		left in		fat		skulled	
\multicolumn{9}{c}{Mental Toughness}
bounce back	/	risks rewarded	/	lapses			
good decisions		risks punished	/	angry swings			
poor decisions		risks safely avoided	/	rushed swings			
\multicolumn{9}{c}{Penalties}
total		OB		lost		water	

Course				Yardage		Date	
			Scoring				
gross		front 9		back 9		net	
eagles		birdies		pars		bogeys	
others		par 3's		par 4's		par 5's	
			Greens in Regulation				
total	/ 18	7I - SW	/	1I - 6I	/	woods	/
			Greens Under Regulation				
attempts		success		par 4's	/	par 5's	/
			Shot-making				
wedges		short irons		mid-irons		long irons	
quality		quality		quality		quality	
fair		fair		fair		fair	
poor		poor		poor		poor	
			Control				
wedges		short irons		mid-irons		long irons	
straight		straight		straight		straight	
left		left		left		left	
right		right		right		right	
			Short Irons / Wedges Hit to Within:				
0' - 10'		10' - 30'		30' +		missed	
			Fairways Hit				
total	/	driver	/	3W - 5W	/	irons	/
			Driving				
quality		straight		solid		short	
fair		left		pulled		hooked	
poor		right		pushed		sliced	

Putting								
total		front 9		back 9		GIR	
1 putts		2 putts		3 putts		per GIR	
One Putts								
inside 5'	/	5' - 10'	/	10' - 20'	/	20' +	/
birdies	/	pars	/	bogeys	/	other	/
Missed Putts								
right		left		short		2' + long	
Long Putts Lagged to Within:								
tap-in		1' - 3'		3' - 5'		5' +	
Chipping								
holed		quality		fair		poor	
Pitching								
holed		quality		fair		poor	
chilly dip		pinched		skulled		fluffed	
Sand Play								
saves		0' - 5'		5' - 10'		10' +	
missed		left in		fat		skulled	
Mental Toughness								
bounce back		/	risks rewarded		/	lapses	
good decisions		risks punished		/	angry swings	
poor decisions		risks safely avoided		/	rushed swings	
Penalties								
total		OB		lost		water	

Course			Yardage		Date	
\multicolumn{7}{|c|}{Scoring}						
gross		front 9		back 9	net	
eagles		birdies		pars	bogeys	
others		par 3's		par 4's	par 5's	
\multicolumn{7}{|c|}{Greens in Regulation}						
total	/ 18	7I - SW	/	1I - 6I	/	woods	/
\multicolumn{7}{|c|}{Greens Under Regulation}						
attempts		success		par 4's	/	par 5's	/
\multicolumn{7}{|c|}{Shot-making}						
wedges		short irons		mid-irons		long irons	
quality		quality		quality		quality	
fair		fair		fair		fair	
poor		poor		poor		poor	
\multicolumn{7}{|c|}{Control}						
wedges		short irons		mid-irons		long irons	
straight		straight		straight		straight	
left		left		left		left	
right		right		right		right	
\multicolumn{7}{|c|}{Short Irons / Wedges Hit to Within:}						
0' - 10'		10' - 30'		30' +		missed	
\multicolumn{7}{|c|}{Fairways Hit}						
total	/	driver	/	3W - 5W	/	irons	/
\multicolumn{7}{|c|}{Driving}						
quality		straight		solid		short	
fair		left		pulled		hooked	
poor		right		pushed		sliced	

Putting								
total		front 9		back 9		GIR	
1 putts		2 putts		3 putts		per GIR	
One Putts								
inside 5'	/	5' - 10'	/	10' - 20'	/	20' +	/
birdies	/	pars	/	bogeys	/	other	/
Missed Putts								
right		left		short		2' + long	
Long Putts Lagged to Within:								
tap-in		1' - 3'		3' - 5'		5' +	
Chipping								
holed		quality		fair		poor	
Pitching								
holed		quality		fair		poor	
chilly dip		pinched		skulled		fluffed	
Sand Play								
saves		0' - 5'		5' - 10'		10' +	
missed		left in		fat		skulled	
Mental Toughness								
bounce back	/	risks rewarded	/	lapses	
good decisions		risks punished	/	angry swings	
poor decisions		risks safely avoided	/	rushed swings	
Penalties								
total		OB		lost		water	

The Golf Stats Log Book

Course				Yardage		Date	
\multicolumn{8}{c}{Scoring}								

Course				Yardage		Date	

Scoring

gross		front 9		back 9		net	
eagles		birdies		pars		bogeys	
others		par 3's		par 4's		par 5's	

Greens in Regulation

total	/ 18	7I - SW	/	1I - 6I	/	woods	/

Greens Under Regulation

attempts		success		par 4's	/	par 5's	/

Shot-making

wedges		short irons		mid-irons		long irons	
quality		quality		quality		quality	
fair		fair		fair		fair	
poor		poor		poor		poor	

Control

wedges		short irons		mid-irons		long irons	
straight		straight		straight		straight	
left		left		left		left	
right		right		right		right	

Short Irons / Wedges Hit to Within:

0' - 10'		10' - 30'		30' +		missed	

Fairways Hit

total	/	driver	/	3W - 5W	/	irons	/

Driving

quality		straight		solid		short	
fair		left		pulled		hooked	
poor		right		pushed		sliced	

Putting							
total		front 9		back 9		GIR	
1 putts		2 putts		3 putts		per GIR	
One Putts							
inside 5'	/	5' - 10'	/	10' - 20'	/	20' +	/
birdies	/	pars	/	bogeys	/	other	/
Missed Putts							
right		left		short		2' + long	
Long Putts Lagged to Within:							
tap-in		1' - 3'		3' - 5'		5' +	
Chipping							
holed		quality		fair		poor	
Pitching							
holed		quality		fair		poor	
chilly dip		pinched		skulled		fluffed	
Sand Play							
saves		0' - 5'		5' - 10'		10' +	
missed		left in		fat		skulled	
Mental Toughness							
bounce back	/	risks rewarded	/	lapses			
good decisions		risks punished	/	angry swings			
poor decisions		risks safely avoided	/	rushed swings			
Penalties							
total		OB		lost		water	

Course			Yardage		Date	
\multicolumn{7}{c}{Scoring}						
gross		front 9		back 9	net	
eagles		birdies		pars	bogeys	
others		par 3's		par 4's	par 5's	
\multicolumn{7}{c}{Greens in Regulation}						
total	/ 18	7I - SW	/	1I - 6I	/	woods	/
\multicolumn{7}{c}{Greens Under Regulation}						
attempts		success		par 4's	/	par 5's	/
\multicolumn{7}{c}{Shot-making}						
wedges		short irons		mid-irons		long irons	
quality		quality		quality		quality	
fair		fair		fair		fair	
poor		poor		poor		poor	
\multicolumn{7}{c}{Control}						
wedges		short irons		mid-irons		long irons	
straight		straight		straight		straight	
left		left		left		left	
right		right		right		right	
\multicolumn{7}{c}{Short Irons / Wedges Hit to Within:}						
0' - 10'		10' - 30'		30' +		missed	
\multicolumn{7}{c}{Fairways Hit}						
total	/	driver	/	3W - 5W	/	irons	/
\multicolumn{7}{c}{Driving}						
quality		straight		solid		short	
fair		left		pulled		hooked	
poor		right		pushed		sliced	

Putting								
total		front 9		back 9		GIR		
1 putts		2 putts		3 putts		per GIR		
One Putts								
inside 5'		/	5' - 10'	/	10' - 20'	/	20' +	/
birdies		/	pars	/	bogeys	/	other	/
Missed Putts								
right		left		short		2' + long		
Long Putts Lagged to Within:								
tap-in		1' - 3'		3' - 5'		5' +		
Chipping								
holed		quality		fair		poor		
Pitching								
holed		quality		fair		poor		
chilly dip		pinched		skulled		fluffed		
Sand Play								
saves		0' - 5'		5' - 10'		10' +		
missed		left in		fat		skulled		
Mental Toughness								
bounce back		/	risks rewarded	/	lapses			
good decisions			risks punished	/	angry swings			
poor decisions			risks safely avoided	/	rushed swings			
Penalties								
total		OB		lost		water		

Course			Yardage		Date	
Scoring							
gross		front 9		back 9		net	
eagles		birdies		pars		bogeys	
others		par 3's		par 4's		par 5's	
Greens in Regulation						
total	/ 18	7I - SW	/	1I - 6I	/	woods	/
Greens Under Regulation						
attempts		success		par 4's	/	par 5's	/
Shot-making						
wedges		short irons		mid-irons		long irons	
quality		quality		quality		quality	
fair		fair		fair		fair	
poor		poor		poor		poor	
Control						
wedges		short irons		mid-irons		long irons	
straight		straight		straight		straight	
left		left		left		left	
right		right		right		right	
Short Irons / Wedges Hit to Within:						
0' - 10'		10' - 30'		30' +		missed	
Fairways Hit						
total	/	driver	/	3W - 5W	/	irons	/
Driving						
quality		straight		solid		short	
fair		left		pulled		hooked	
poor		right		pushed		sliced	

Putting							
total		front 9		back 9		GIR	
1 putts		2 putts		3 putts		per GIR	
One Putts							
inside 5'	/	5' - 10'	/	10' - 20'	/	20' +	/
birdies	/	pars	/	bogeys	/	other	/
Missed Putts							
right		left		short		2' + long	
Long Putts Lagged to Within:							
tap-in		1' - 3'		3' - 5'		5' +	
Chipping							
holed		quality		fair		poor	
Pitching							
holed		quality		fair		poor	
chilly dip		pinched		skulled		fluffed	
Sand Play							
saves		0' - 5'		5' - 10'		10' +	
missed		left in		fat		skulled	
Mental Toughness							
bounce back	/	risks rewarded	/	lapses			
good decisions		risks punished	/	angry swings			
poor decisions		risks safely avoided	/	rushed swings			
Penalties							
total		OB		lost		water	

Course				Yardage		Date	
\multicolumn{8}{c}{Scoring}						
gross		front 9		back 9		net	
eagles		birdies		pars		bogeys	
others		par 3's		par 4's		par 5's	
\multicolumn{8}{c}{Greens in Regulation}						
total	/ 18	7I - SW	/	1I - 6I	/	woods	/
\multicolumn{8}{c}{Greens Under Regulation}						
attempts		success		par 4's	/	par 5's	/
\multicolumn{8}{c}{Shot-making}						
wedges		short irons		mid-irons		long irons	
quality		quality		quality		quality	
fair		fair		fair		fair	
poor		poor		poor		poor	
\multicolumn{8}{c}{Control}						
wedges		short irons		mid-irons		long irons	
straight		straight		straight		straight	
left		left		left		left	
right		right		right		right	
\multicolumn{8}{c}{Short Irons / Wedges Hit to Within:}						
0' - 10'		10' - 30'		30' +		missed	
\multicolumn{8}{c}{Fairways Hit}						
total	/	driver	/	3W - 5W	/	irons	/
\multicolumn{8}{c}{Driving}						
quality		straight		solid		short	
fair		left		pulled		hooked	
poor		right		pushed		sliced	

The Golf Stats Log Book

Putting						
total		front 9		back 9		GIR	
1 putts		2 putts		3 putts		per GIR	
One Putts						
inside 5'	/	5' - 10'	/	10' - 20'	/	20' +	/
birdies	/	pars	/	bogeys	/	other	/
Missed Putts						
right		left		short		2' + long	
Long Putts Lagged to Within:						
tap-in		1' - 3'		3' - 5'		5' +	
Chipping						
holed		quality		fair		poor	
Pitching						
holed		quality		fair		poor	
chilly dip		pinched		skulled		fluffed	
Sand Play						
saves		0' - 5'		5' - 10'		10' +	
missed		left in		fat		skulled	
Mental Toughness						
bounce back	/	risks rewarded	/	lapses			
good decisions		risks punished	/	angry swings			
poor decisions		risks safely avoided	/	rushed swings			
Penalties						
total		OB		lost		water	

Course			Yardage		Date	
	Scoring					
gross		front 9		back 9	net	
eagles		birdies		pars	bogeys	
others		par 3's		par 4's	par 5's	

	Greens in Regulation						
total		/ 18	7I - SW	/	1I - 6I	/	woods	/

Greens in Regulation

total		/ 18	7I - SW	/	1I - 6I	/	woods	/

Greens Under Regulation

attempts		success		par 4's	/	par 5's	/

Shot-making

wedges		short irons		mid-irons		long irons	
quality		quality		quality		quality	
fair		fair		fair		fair	
poor		poor		poor		poor	

Control

wedges		short irons		mid-irons		long irons	
straight		straight		straight		straight	
left		left		left		left	
right		right		right		right	

Short Irons / Wedges Hit to Within:

0' - 10'		10' - 30'		30' +		missed	

Fairways Hit

total		/	driver	/	3W - 5W	/	irons	/

Driving

quality		straight		solid		short	
fair		left		pulled		hooked	
poor		right		pushed		sliced	

Putting							
total		front 9		back 9		GIR	
1 putts		2 putts		3 putts		per GIR	
One Putts							
inside 5'	/	5' - 10'	/	10' - 20'	/	20' +	/
birdies	/	pars	/	bogeys	/	other	/
Missed Putts							
right		left		short		2' + long	
Long Putts Lagged to Within:							
tap-in		1' - 3'		3' - 5'		5' +	
Chipping							
holed		quality		fair		poor	
Pitching							
holed		quality		fair		poor	
chilly dip		pinched		skulled		fluffed	
Sand Play							
saves		0' - 5'		5' - 10'		10' +	
missed		left in		fat		skulled	
Mental Toughness							
bounce back	/	risks rewarded	/	lapses			
good decisions		risks punished	/	angry swings			
poor decisions		risks safely avoided	/	rushed swings			
Penalties							
total		OB		lost		water	

Course				Yardage		Date	
\multicolumn{8}{c}{Scoring}						
gross		front 9		back 9		net	
eagles		birdies		pars		bogeys	
others		par 3's		par 4's		par 5's	
\multicolumn{8}{c}{Greens in Regulation}						
total	/ 18	7I - SW	/	1I - 6I	/	woods	/
\multicolumn{8}{c}{Greens Under Regulation}						
attempts		success		par 4's	/	par 5's	/
\multicolumn{8}{c}{Shot-making}						
wedges		short irons		mid-irons		long irons	
quality		quality		quality		quality	
fair		fair		fair		fair	
poor		poor		poor		poor	
\multicolumn{8}{c}{Control}						
wedges		short irons		mid-irons		long irons	
straight		straight		straight		straight	
left		left		left		left	
right		right		right		right	
\multicolumn{8}{c}{Short Irons / Wedges Hit to Within:}						
0' - 10'		10' - 30'		30' +		missed	
\multicolumn{8}{c}{Fairways Hit}						
total	/	driver	/	3W - 5W	/	irons	/
\multicolumn{8}{c}{Driving}						
quality		straight		solid		short	
fair		left		pulled		hooked	
poor		right		pushed		sliced	

Putting								
total		front 9		back 9		GIR	
1 putts		2 putts		3 putts		per GIR	
One Putts								
inside 5'	/	5' - 10'	/	10' - 20'	/	20' +	/
birdies	/	pars	/	bogeys	/	other	/
Missed Putts								
right		left		short		2' + long	
Long Putts Lagged to Within:								
tap-in		1' - 3'		3' - 5'		5' +	
Chipping								
holed		quality		fair		poor	
Pitching								
holed		quality		fair		poor	
chilly dip		pinched		skulled		fluffed	
Sand Play								
saves		0' - 5'		5' - 10'		10' +	
missed		left in		fat		skulled	
Mental Toughness								
bounce back	/	risks rewarded	/	lapses	
good decisions		risks punished	/	angry swings	
poor decisions		risks safely avoided	/	rushed swings	
Penalties								
total		OB		lost		water	

Course				Yardage		Date	
\multicolumn{8}{c}{Scoring}						
gross		front 9		back 9		net	
eagles		birdies		pars		bogeys	
others		par 3's		par 4's		par 5's	
\multicolumn{8}{c}{Greens in Regulation}						
total	/ 18	7I - SW	/	1I - 6I	/	woods	/
\multicolumn{8}{c}{Greens Under Regulation}						
attempts		success		par 4's	/	par 5's	/
\multicolumn{8}{c}{Shot-making}						
wedges		short irons		mid-irons		long irons	
quality		quality		quality		quality	
fair		fair		fair		fair	
poor		poor		poor		poor	
\multicolumn{8}{c}{Control}						
wedges		short irons		mid-irons		long irons	
straight		straight		straight		straight	
left		left		left		left	
right		right		right		right	
\multicolumn{8}{c}{Short Irons / Wedges Hit to Within:}						
0' - 10'		10' - 30'		30' +		missed	
\multicolumn{8}{c}{Fairways Hit}						
total	/	driver	/	3W - 5W	/	irons	/
\multicolumn{8}{c}{Driving}						
quality		straight		solid		short	
fair		left		pulled		hooked	
poor		right		pushed		sliced	

Putting								
total		front 9		back 9		GIR	
1 putts		2 putts		3 putts		per GIR	
One Putts								
inside 5'		/	5' - 10'	/	10' - 20'	/	20' +	/
birdies		/	pars	/	bogeys	/	other	/
Missed Putts								
right		left		short		2' + long	
Long Putts Lagged to Within:								
tap-in		1' - 3'		3' - 5'		5' +	
Chipping								
holed		quality		fair		poor	
Pitching								
holed		quality		fair		poor	
chilly dip		pinched		skulled		fluffed	
Sand Play								
saves		0' - 5'		5' - 10'		10' +	
missed		left in		fat		skulled	
Mental Toughness								
bounce back		/	risks rewarded	/	lapses		
good decisions		risks punished		/	angry swings		
poor decisions		risks safely avoided		/	rushed swings		
Penalties								
total		OB		lost		water	

The Golf Stats Log Book

Course				Yardage		Date	
Scoring							
gross		front 9		back 9		net	
eagles		birdies		pars		bogeys	
others		par 3's		par 4's		par 5's	
Greens in Regulation							
total	/ 18	7I - SW	/	1I - 6I	/	woods	/
Greens Under Regulation							
attempts		success		par 4's	/	par 5's	/
Shot-making							
wedges		short irons		mid-irons		long irons	
quality		quality		quality		quality	
fair		fair		fair		fair	
poor		poor		poor		poor	
Control							
wedges		short irons		mid-irons		long irons	
straight		straight		straight		straight	
left		left		left		left	
right		right		right		right	
Short Irons / Wedges Hit to Within:							
0' - 10'		10' - 30'		30' +		missed	
Fairways Hit							
total	/	driver	/	3W - 5W	/	irons	/
Driving							
quality		straight		solid		short	
fair		left		pulled		hooked	
poor		right		pushed		sliced	

The Golf Stats Log Book

Putting							
total		front 9		back 9		GIR	
1 putts		2 putts		3 putts		per GIR	
One Putts							
inside 5'	/	5' - 10'	/	10' - 20'	/	20' +	/
birdies	/	pars	/	bogeys	/	other	/
Missed Putts							
right		left		short		2' + long	
Long Putts Lagged to Within:							
tap-in		1' - 3'		3' - 5'		5' +	
Chipping							
holed		quality		fair		poor	
Pitching							
holed		quality		fair		poor	
chilly dip		pinched		skulled		fluffed	
Sand Play							
saves		0' - 5'		5' - 10'		10' +	
missed		left in		fat		skulled	
Mental Toughness							
bounce back	/	risks rewarded	/	lapses			
good decisions		risks punished	/	angry swings			
poor decisions		risks safely avoided	/	rushed swings			
Penalties							
total		OB		lost		water	

Course			Yardage		Date	
\multicolumn{7}{c}{Scoring}						

Course			Yardage		Date	

Scoring

gross		front 9		back 9		net	
eagles		birdies		pars		bogeys	
others		par 3's		par 4's		par 5's	

Greens in Regulation

total	/ 18	7I - SW	/	1I - 6I	/	woods	/

Greens Under Regulation

attempts		success		par 4's	/	par 5's	/

Shot-making

wedges		short irons		mid-irons		long irons	
quality		quality		quality		quality	
fair		fair		fair		fair	
poor		poor		poor		poor	

Control

wedges		short irons		mid-irons		long irons	
straight		straight		straight		straight	
left		left		left		left	
right		right		right		right	

Short Irons / Wedges Hit to Within:

0' - 10'		10' - 30'		30' +		missed	

Fairways Hit

total	/	driver	/	3W - 5W	/	irons	/

Driving

quality		straight		solid		short	
fair		left		pulled		hooked	
poor		right		pushed		sliced	

	Putting								
total		front 9		back 9		GIR	
1 putts		2 putts		3 putts		per GIR	
	One Putts								
inside 5'	/	5' - 10'	/	10' - 20'	/	20' +	/
birdies	/	pars	/	bogeys	/	other	/
	Missed Putts								
right		left		short		2' + long	
	Long Putts Lagged to Within:								
tap-in		1' - 3'		3' - 5'		5' +	
	Chipping								
holed		quality		fair		poor	
	Pitching								
holed		quality		fair		poor	
chilly dip		pinched		skulled		fluffed	
	Sand Play								
saves		0' - 5'		5' - 10'		10' +	
missed		left in		fat		skulled	
	Mental Toughness								
bounce back	/	risks rewarded	/	lapses	
good decisions		risks punished	/	angry swings	
poor decisions		risks safely avoided	/	rushed swings	
	Penalties								
total		OB		lost		water	

The Golf Stats Log Book

Course				Yardage		Date	
Scoring							
gross		front 9		back 9		net	
eagles		birdies		pars		bogeys	
others		par 3's		par 4's		par 5's	
Greens in Regulation							
total	/ 18	7I - SW	/	1I - 6I	/	woods	/
Greens Under Regulation							
attempts		success		par 4's	/	par 5's	/
Shot-making							
wedges		short irons		mid-irons		long irons	
quality		quality		quality		quality	
fair		fair		fair		fair	
poor		poor		poor		poor	
Control							
wedges		short irons		mid-irons		long irons	
straight		straight		straight		straight	
left		left		left		left	
right		right		right		right	
Short Irons / Wedges Hit to Within:							
0' - 10'		10' - 30'		30' +		missed	
Fairways Hit							
total	/	driver	/	3W - 5W	/	irons	/
Driving							
quality		straight		solid		short	
fair		left		pulled		hooked	
poor		right		pushed		sliced	

34

Putting								
total		front 9		back 9		GIR	
1 putts		2 putts		3 putts		per GIR	
One Putts								
inside 5'	/	5' - 10'	/	10' - 20'	/	20' +	/
birdies	/	pars	/	bogeys	/	other	/
Missed Putts								
right		left		short		2' + long	
Long Putts Lagged to Within:								
tap-in		1' - 3'		3' - 5'		5' +	
Chipping								
holed		quality		fair		poor	
Pitching								
holed		quality		fair		poor	
chilly dip		pinched		skulled		fluffed	
Sand Play								
saves		0' - 5'		5' - 10'		10' +	
missed		left in		fat		skulled	
Mental Toughness								
bounce back	/	risks rewarded	/	lapses	
good decisions		risks punished	/	angry swings	
poor decisions		risks safely avoided	/	rushed swings	
Penalties								
total		OB		lost		water	

Course				Yardage		Date	
\multicolumn{8}{c}{Scoring}								
gross		front 9		back 9		net	
eagles		birdies		pars		bogeys	
others		par 3's		par 4's		par 5's	
\multicolumn{8}{c}{Greens in Regulation}								
total	/ 18	7I - SW	/	1I - 6I	/	woods	/
\multicolumn{8}{c}{Greens Under Regulation}								
attempts		success		par 4's	/	par 5's	/
\multicolumn{8}{c}{Shot-making}								
wedges		short irons		mid-irons		long irons	
quality		quality		quality		quality	
fair		fair		fair		fair	
poor		poor		poor		poor	
\multicolumn{8}{c}{Control}								
wedges		short irons		mid-irons		long irons	
straight		straight		straight		straight	
left		left		left		left	
right		right		right		right	
\multicolumn{8}{c}{Short Irons / Wedges Hit to Within:}								
0' - 10'		10' - 30'		30' +		missed	
\multicolumn{8}{c}{Fairways Hit}								
total	/	driver	/	3W - 5W	/	irons	/
\multicolumn{8}{c}{Driving}								
quality		straight		solid		short	
fair		left		pulled		hooked	
poor		right		pushed		sliced	

Putting								
total		front 9		back 9		GIR	
1 putts		2 putts		3 putts		per GIR	
One Putts								
inside 5'		/	5' - 10'		/	10' - 20'		/	20' +		/
birdies		/	pars		/	bogeys		/	other		/
Missed Putts								
right		left		short		2' + long	
Long Putts Lagged to Within:								
tap-in		1' - 3'		3' - 5'		5' +	
Chipping								
holed		quality		fair		poor	
Pitching								
holed		quality		fair		poor	
chilly dip		pinched		skulled		fluffed	
Sand Play								
saves		0' - 5'		5' - 10'		10' +	
missed		left in		fat		skulled	
Mental Toughness								
bounce back		/	risks rewarded		/	lapses	
good decisions		risks punished		/	angry swings	
poor decisions		risks safely avoided		/	rushed swings	
Penalties								
total		OB		lost		water	

Course				Yardage		Date	
Scoring								
gross		front 9		back 9		net	
eagles		birdies		pars		bogeys	
others		par 3's		par 4's		par 5's	
Greens in Regulation								
total	/ 18	7I - SW	/	1I - 6I	/	woods	/
Greens Under Regulation								
attempts		success		par 4's	/	par 5's	/
Shot-making								
wedges		short irons		mid-irons		long irons	
quality		quality		quality		quality	
fair		fair		fair		fair	
poor		poor		poor		poor	
Control								
wedges		short irons		mid-irons		long irons	
straight		straight		straight		straight	
left		left		left		left	
right		right		right		right	
Short Irons / Wedges Hit to Within:								
0' - 10'		10' - 30'		30' +		missed	
Fairways Hit								
total	/	driver	/	3W - 5W	/	irons	/
Driving								
quality		straight		solid		short	
fair		left		pulled		hooked	
poor		right		pushed		sliced	

Putting								
total		front 9		back 9		GIR		
1 putts		2 putts		3 putts		per GIR		
One Putts								
inside 5'		/	5' - 10'	/	10' - 20'	/	20' +	/
birdies		/	pars	/	bogeys	/	other	/
Missed Putts								
right		left		short		2' + long		
Long Putts Lagged to Within:								
tap-in		1' - 3'		3' - 5'		5' +		
Chipping								
holed		quality		fair		poor		
Pitching								
holed		quality		fair		poor		
chilly dip		pinched		skulled		fluffed		
Sand Play								
saves		0' - 5'		5' - 10'		10' +		
missed		left in		fat		skulled		
Mental Toughness								
bounce back		/	risks rewarded	/	lapses			
good decisions			risks punished	/	angry swings			
poor decisions			risks safely avoided	/	rushed swings			
Penalties								
total		OB		lost		water		

Course				Yardage		Date	
Scoring								

gross		front 9		back 9		net	
eagles		birdies		pars		bogeys	
others		par 3's		par 4's		par 5's	

Greens in Regulation

total	/ 18	7I - SW	/	1I - 6I	/	woods	/

Greens Under Regulation

attempts		success		par 4's	/	par 5's	/

Shot-making

wedges		short irons		mid-irons		long irons	
quality		quality		quality		quality	
fair		fair		fair		fair	
poor		poor		poor		poor	

Control

wedges		short irons		mid-irons		long irons	
straight		straight		straight		straight	
left		left		left		left	
right		right		right		right	

Short Irons / Wedges Hit to Within:

0' - 10'		10' - 30'		30' +		missed	

Fairways Hit

total	/	driver	/	3W - 5W	/	irons	/

Driving

quality		straight		solid		short	
fair		left		pulled		hooked	
poor		right		pushed		sliced	

Putting								
total		front 9		back 9		GIR	
1 putts		2 putts		3 putts		per GIR	
One Putts								
inside 5'		/	5' - 10'	/	10' - 20'	/	20' +	/
birdies		/	pars	/	bogeys	/	other	/
Missed Putts								
right		left		short		2' + long	
Long Putts Lagged to Within:								
tap-in		1' - 3'		3' - 5'		5' +	
Chipping								
holed		quality		fair		poor	
Pitching								
holed		quality		fair		poor	
chilly dip		pinched		skulled		fluffed	
Sand Play								
saves		0' - 5'		5' - 10'		10' +	
missed		left in		fat		skulled	
Mental Toughness								
bounce back		/	risks rewarded	/	lapses	
good decisions			risks punished	/	angry swings	
poor decisions			risks safely avoided	/	rushed swings	
Penalties								
total		OB		lost		water	

Course				Yardage		Date	
Scoring							
gross		front 9		back 9		net	
eagles		birdies		pars		bogeys	
others		par 3's		par 4's		par 5's	
Greens in Regulation							
total	/ 18	7I - SW	/	1I - 6I	/	woods	/
Greens Under Regulation							
attempts		success		par 4's	/	par 5's	/
Shot-making							
wedges		short irons		mid-irons		long irons	
quality		quality		quality		quality	
fair		fair		fair		fair	
poor		poor		poor		poor	
Control							
wedges		short irons		mid-irons		long irons	
straight		straight		straight		straight	
left		left		left		left	
right		right		right		right	
Short Irons / Wedges Hit to Within:							
0' - 10'		10' - 30'		30' +		missed	
Fairways Hit							
total	/	driver	/	3W - 5W	/	irons	/
Driving							
quality		straight		solid		short	
fair		left		pulled		hooked	
poor		right		pushed		sliced	

The Golf Stats Log Book

Putting								
total		front 9		back 9		GIR		
1 putts		2 putts		3 putts		per GIR		
One Putts								
inside 5'		5' - 10'	/	10' - 20'	/	20' +	/	
birdies	/	pars	/	bogeys	/	other	/	
Missed Putts								
right		left		short		2' + long		
Long Putts Lagged to Within:								
tap-in		1' - 3'		3' - 5'		5' +		
Chipping								
holed		quality		fair		poor		
Pitching								
holed		quality		fair		poor		
chilly dip		pinched		skulled		fluffed		
Sand Play								
saves		0' - 5'		5' - 10'		10' +		
missed		left in		fat		skulled		
Mental Toughness								
bounce back		/	risks rewarded		/	lapses		
good decisions			risks punished		/	angry swings		
poor decisions			risks safely avoided		/	rushed swings		
Penalties								
total		OB		lost		water		

43

Course				Yardage		Date	
Scoring							
gross		front 9		back 9		net	
eagles		birdies		pars		bogeys	
others		par 3's		par 4's		par 5's	
Greens in Regulation							
total	/ 18	7I - SW	/	1I - 6I	/	woods	/
Greens Under Regulation							
attempts		success		par 4's	/	par 5's	/
Shot-making							
wedges		short irons		mid-irons		long irons	
quality		quality		quality		quality	
fair		fair		fair		fair	
poor		poor		poor		poor	
Control							
wedges		short irons		mid-irons		long irons	
straight		straight		straight		straight	
left		left		left		left	
right		right		right		right	
Short Irons / Wedges Hit to Within:							
0' - 10'		10' - 30'		30' +		missed	
Fairways Hit							
total	/	driver	/	3W - 5W	/	irons	/
Driving							
quality		straight		solid		short	
fair		left		pulled		hooked	
poor		right		pushed		sliced	

The Golf Stats Log Book

Putting							
total		front 9		back 9		GIR	
1 putts		2 putts		3 putts		per GIR	
One Putts							
inside 5'	/	5' - 10'	/	10' - 20'	/	20' +	/
birdies	/	pars	/	bogeys	/	other	/
Missed Putts							
right		left		short		2' + long	
Long Putts Lagged to Within:							
tap-in		1' - 3'		3' - 5'		5' +	
Chipping							
holed		quality		fair		poor	
Pitching							
holed		quality		fair		poor	
chilly dip		pinched		skulled		fluffed	
Sand Play							
saves		0' - 5'		5' - 10'		10' +	
missed		left in		fat		skulled	
Mental Toughness							
bounce back	/	risks rewarded	/	lapses			
good decisions		risks punished	/	angry swings			
poor decisions		risks safely avoided	/	rushed swings			
Penalties							
total		OB		lost		water	

Course				Yardage		Date	
\multicolumn{8}{c}{Scoring}						
gross		front 9		back 9		net	
eagles		birdies		pars		bogeys	
others		par 3's		par 4's		par 5's	
\multicolumn{8}{c}{Greens in Regulation}						
total		/ 18	7I - SW	/	1I - 6I	/	woods	/
\multicolumn{8}{c}{Greens Under Regulation}						
attempts		success		par 4's	/	par 5's	/
\multicolumn{8}{c}{Shot-making}						
wedges		short irons		mid-irons		long irons	
quality		quality		quality		quality	
fair		fair		fair		fair	
poor		poor		poor		poor	
\multicolumn{8}{c}{Control}						
wedges		short irons		mid-irons		long irons	
straight		straight		straight		straight	
left		left		left		left	
right		right		right		right	
\multicolumn{8}{c}{Short Irons / Wedges Hit to Within:}						
0' - 10'		10' - 30'		30' +		missed	
\multicolumn{8}{c}{Fairways Hit}						
total	/	driver	/	3W - 5W	/	irons	/
\multicolumn{8}{c}{Driving}						
quality		straight		solid		short	
fair		left		pulled		hooked	
poor		right		pushed		sliced	

Putting								
total		front 9		back 9		GIR	
1 putts		2 putts		3 putts		per GIR	
One Putts								
inside 5'		/	5' - 10'	/	10' - 20'	/	20' +	/
birdies		/	pars	/	bogeys	/	other	/
Missed Putts								
right		left		short		2' + long	
Long Putts Lagged to Within:								
tap-in		1' - 3'		3' - 5'		5' +	
Chipping								
holed		quality		fair		poor	
Pitching								
holed		quality		fair		poor	
chilly dip		pinched		skulled		fluffed	
Sand Play								
saves		0' - 5'		5' - 10'		10' +	
missed		left in		fat		skulled	
Mental Toughness								
bounce back		/	risks rewarded	/	lapses	
good decisions			risks punished	/	angry swings	
poor decisions			risks safely avoided	/	rushed swings	
Penalties								
total		OB		lost		water	

Course				Yardage		Date	
\multicolumn{8}{c}{Scoring}							

Course				Yardage		Date	

Scoring

gross		front 9		back 9		net	
eagles		birdies		pars		bogeys	
others		par 3's		par 4's		par 5's	

Greens in Regulation

total	/ 18	7I - SW	/	1I - 6I	/	woods	/

Greens Under Regulation

attempts		success		par 4's	/	par 5's	/

Shot-making

wedges		short irons		mid-irons		long irons	
quality		quality		quality		quality	
fair		fair		fair		fair	
poor		poor		poor		poor	

Control

wedges		short irons		mid-irons		long irons	
straight		straight		straight		straight	
left		left		left		left	
right		right		right		right	

Short Irons / Wedges Hit to Within:

0' - 10'		10' - 30'		30' +		missed	

Fairways Hit

total	/	driver	/	3W - 5W	/	irons	/

Driving

quality		straight		solid		short	
fair		left		pulled		hooked	
poor		right		pushed		sliced	

Putting								
total		front 9		back 9		GIR		
1 putts		2 putts		3 putts		per GIR		
One Putts								
inside 5'	/	5' - 10'	/	10' - 20'	/	20' +	/	
birdies	/	pars	/	bogeys	/	other	/	
Missed Putts								
right		left		short		2' + long		
Long Putts Lagged to Within:								
tap-in		1' - 3'		3' - 5'		5' +		
Chipping								
holed		quality		fair		poor		
Pitching								
holed		quality		fair		poor		
chilly dip		pinched		skulled		fluffed		
Sand Play								
saves		0' - 5'		5' - 10'		10' +		
missed		left in		fat		skulled		
Mental Toughness								
bounce back	/	risks rewarded	/	lapses				
good decisions		risks punished	/	angry swings				
poor decisions		risks safely avoided	/	rushed swings				
Penalties								
total		OB		lost		water		

Course			Yardage		Date	
Scoring							
gross		front 9		back 9		net	
eagles		birdies		pars		bogeys	
others		par 3's		par 4's		par 5's	
Greens in Regulation							
total	/ 18	7I - SW	/	1I - 6I	/	woods	/
Greens Under Regulation							
attempts		success		par 4's	/	par 5's	/
Shot-making							
wedges		short irons		mid-irons		long irons	
quality		quality		quality		quality	
fair		fair		fair		fair	
poor		poor		poor		poor	
Control							
wedges		short irons		mid-irons		long irons	
straight		straight		straight		straight	
left		left		left		left	
right		right		right		right	
Short Irons / Wedges Hit to Within:							
0' - 10'		10' - 30'		30' +		missed	
Fairways Hit							
total	/	driver	/	3W - 5W	/	irons	/
Driving							
quality		straight		solid		short	
fair		left		pulled		hooked	
poor		right		pushed		sliced	

Putting								
total		front 9		back 9		GIR	
1 putts		2 putts		3 putts		per GIR	
One Putts								
inside 5'	/	5' - 10'	/	10' - 20'	/	20' +	/
birdies	/	pars	/	bogeys	/	other	/
Missed Putts								
right		left		short		2' + long	
Long Putts Lagged to Within:								
tap-in		1' - 3'		3' - 5'		5' +	
Chipping								
holed		quality		fair		poor	
Pitching								
holed		quality		fair		poor	
chilly dip		pinched		skulled		fluffed	
Sand Play								
saves		0' - 5'		5' - 10'		10' +	
missed		left in		fat		skulled	
Mental Toughness								
bounce back	/	risks rewarded	/	lapses	
good decisions		risks punished	/	angry swings	
poor decisions		risks safely avoided	/	rushed swings	
Penalties								
total		OB		lost		water	

Course				Yardage		Date	
Scoring							
gross		front 9		back 9		net	
eagles		birdies		pars		bogeys	
others		par 3's		par 4's		par 5's	
Greens in Regulation							
total	/ 18	7I - SW	/	1I - 6I	/	woods	/
Greens Under Regulation							
attempts		success		par 4's	/	par 5's	/
Shot-making							
wedges		short irons		mid-irons		long irons	
quality		quality		quality		quality	
fair		fair		fair		fair	
poor		poor		poor		poor	
Control							
wedges		short irons		mid-irons		long irons	
straight		straight		straight		straight	
left		left		left		left	
right		right		right		right	
Short Irons / Wedges Hit to Within:							
0' - 10'		10' - 30'		30' +		missed	
Fairways Hit							
total	/	driver	/	3W - 5W	/	irons	/
Driving							
quality		straight		solid		short	
fair		left		pulled		hooked	
poor		right		pushed		sliced	

The Golf Stats Log Book

Putting								
total		front 9		back 9		GIR	
1 putts		2 putts		3 putts		per GIR	
One Putts								
inside 5'		/	5' - 10'	/	10' - 20'	/	20' +	/
birdies		/	pars	/	bogeys	/	other	/
Missed Putts								
right		left		short		2' + long	
Long Putts Lagged to Within:								
tap-in		1' - 3'		3' - 5'		5' +	
Chipping								
holed		quality		fair		poor	
Pitching								
holed		quality		fair		poor	
chilly dip		pinched		skulled		fluffed	
Sand Play								
saves		0' - 5'		5' - 10'		10' +	
missed		left in		fat		skulled	
Mental Toughness								
bounce back		/	risks rewarded	/	lapses	
good decisions			risks punished	/	angry swings	
poor decisions			risks safely avoided	/	rushed swings	
Penalties								
total		OB		lost		water	

Course				Yardage		Date	
\multicolumn{8}{c}{Scoring}								
gross		front 9		back 9		net	
eagles		birdies		pars		bogeys	
others		par 3's		par 4's		par 5's	
\multicolumn{8}{c}{Greens in Regulation}								
total	/ 18	7I - SW	/	1I - 6I	/	woods	/
\multicolumn{8}{c}{Greens Under Regulation}								
attempts		success		par 4's	/	par 5's	/
\multicolumn{8}{c}{Shot-making}								
wedges		short irons		mid-irons		long irons	
quality		quality		quality		quality	
fair		fair		fair		fair	
poor		poor		poor		poor	
\multicolumn{8}{c}{Control}								
wedges		short irons		mid-irons		long irons	
straight		straight		straight		straight	
left		left		left		left	
right		right		right		right	
\multicolumn{8}{c}{Short Irons / Wedges Hit to Within:}								
0' - 10'		10' - 30'		30' +		missed	
\multicolumn{8}{c}{Fairways Hit}								
total	/	driver	/	3W - 5W	/	irons	/
\multicolumn{8}{c}{Driving}								
quality		straight		solid		short	
fair		left		pulled		hooked	
poor		right		pushed		sliced	

The Golf Stats Log

Putting							
total		front 9		back 9		GIR	
1 putts		2 putts		3 putts		per GIR	
One Putts							
inside 5'	/	5' - 10'	/	10' - 20'	/	20' +	/
birdies	/	pars	/	bogeys	/	other	/
Missed Putts							
right		left		short		2' + long	
Long Putts Lagged to Within:							
tap-in		1' - 3'		3' - 5'		5' +	
Chipping							
holed		quality		fair		poor	
Pitching							
holed		quality		fair		poor	
chilly dip		pinched		skulled		fluffed	
Sand Play							
saves		0' - 5'		5' - 10'		10' +	
missed		left in		fat		skulled	
Mental Toughness							
bounce back	/	risks rewarded	/	lapses			
good decisions		risks punished	/	angry swings			
poor decisions		risks safely avoided	/	rushed swings			
Penalties							
total		OB		lost		water	

Course				Yardage		Date	
Scoring							
gross		front 9		back 9		net	
eagles		birdies		pars		bogeys	
others		par 3's		par 4's		par 5's	
Greens in Regulation							
total		/ 18	7I - SW	/	1I - 6I	/	woods	/
Greens Under Regulation							
attempts		success		par 4's	/	par 5's	/
Shot-making							
wedges		short irons		mid-irons		long irons	
quality		quality		quality		quality	
fair		fair		fair		fair	
poor		poor		poor		poor	
Control							
wedges		short irons		mid-irons		long irons	
straight		straight		straight		straight	
left		left		left		left	
right		right		right		right	
Short Irons / Wedges Hit to Within:							
0' - 10'		10' - 30'		30' +		missed	
Fairways Hit							
total		/	driver	/	3W - 5W	/	irons	/
Driving							
quality		straight		solid		short	
fair		left		pulled		hooked	
poor		right		pushed		sliced	

\multicolumn{8}{c}{Putting}							
total		front 9		back 9		GIR	
1 putts		2 putts		3 putts		per GIR	
\multicolumn{8}{c}{One Putts}							
inside 5'	/	5' - 10'	/	10' - 20'	/	20' +	/
birdies	/	pars	/	bogeys	/	other	/
\multicolumn{8}{c}{Missed Putts}							
right		left		short		2' + long	
\multicolumn{8}{c}{Long Putts Lagged to Within:}							
tap-in		1' - 3'		3' - 5'		5' +	
\multicolumn{8}{c}{Chipping}							
holed		quality		fair		poor	
\multicolumn{8}{c}{Pitching}							
holed		quality		fair		poor	
chilly dip		pinched		skulled		fluffed	
\multicolumn{8}{c}{Sand Play}							
saves		0' - 5'		5' - 10'		10' +	
missed		left in		fat		skulled	
\multicolumn{8}{c}{Mental Toughness}							
bounce back	/	risks rewarded	/	lapses			
good decisions		risks punished	/	angry swings			
poor decisions		risks safely avoided	/	rushed swings			
\multicolumn{8}{c}{Penalties}							
total		OB		lost		water	

Course			Yardage		Date	

Scoring							
gross		front 9		back 9		net	
eagles		birdies		pars		bogeys	
others		par 3's		par 4's		par 5's	

Greens in Regulation							
total	/ 18	7I - SW	/	1I - 6I	/	woods	/

Greens Under Regulation							
attempts		success		par 4's	/	par 5's	/

Shot-making							
wedges		short irons		mid-irons		long irons	
quality		quality		quality		quality	
fair		fair		fair		fair	
poor		poor		poor		poor	

Control							
wedges		short irons		mid-irons		long irons	
straight		straight		straight		straight	
left		left		left		left	
right		right		right		right	

Short Irons / Wedges Hit to Within:							
0' - 10'		10' - 30'		30' +		missed	

Fairways Hit							
total	/	driver	/	3W - 5W	/	irons	/

Driving							
quality		straight		solid		short	
fair		left		pulled		hooked	
poor		right		pushed		sliced	

The Golf Stats Log Book

Putting							
total		front 9		back 9		GIR	
1 putts		2 putts		3 putts		per GIR	
One Putts							
inside 5'	/	5' - 10'	/	10' - 20'	/	20' +	/
birdies	/	pars	/	bogeys	/	other	/
Missed Putts							
right		left		short		2' + long	
Long Putts Lagged to Within:							
tap-in		1' - 3'		3' - 5'		5' +	
Chipping							
holed		quality		fair		poor	
Pitching							
holed		quality		fair		poor	
chilly dip		pinched		skulled		fluffed	
Sand Play							
saves		0' - 5'		5' - 10'		10' +	
missed		left in		fat		skulled	
Mental Toughness							
bounce back	/	risks rewarded	/	lapses			
good decisions		risks punished	/	angry swings			
poor decisions		risks safely avoided	/	rushed swings			
Penalties							
total		OB		lost		water	

59

Course				Yardage		Date	
Scoring								
gross		front 9		back 9		net	
eagles		birdies		pars		bogeys	
others		par 3's		par 4's		par 5's	
Greens in Regulation								
total	/ 18	7I - SW	/	1I - 6I	/	woods	/
Greens Under Regulation								
attempts		success		par 4's	/	par 5's	/
Shot-making								
wedges		short irons		mid-irons		long irons	
quality		quality		quality		quality	
fair		fair		fair		fair	
poor		poor		poor		poor	
Control								
wedges		short irons		mid-irons		long irons	
straight		straight		straight		straight	
left		left		left		left	
right		right		right		right	
Short Irons / Wedges Hit to Within:								
0' - 10'		10' - 30'		30' +		missed	
Fairways Hit								
total	/	driver	/	3W - 5W	/	irons	/
Driving								
quality		straight		solid		short	
fair		left		pulled		hooked	
poor		right		pushed		sliced	

Putting							
total		front 9		back 9		GIR	
1 putts		2 putts		3 putts		per GIR	
One Putts							
inside 5'	/	5' - 10'	/	10' - 20'	/	20' +	/
birdies	/	pars	/	bogeys	/	other	/
Missed Putts							
right		left		short		2' + long	
Long Putts Lagged to Within:							
tap-in		1' - 3'		3' - 5'		5' +	
Chipping							
holed		quality		fair		poor	
Pitching							
holed		quality		fair		poor	
chilly dip		pinched		skulled		fluffed	
Sand Play							
saves		0' - 5'		5' - 10'		10' +	
missed		left in		fat		skulled	
Mental Toughness							
bounce back	/	risks rewarded	/	lapses			
good decisions		risks punished	/	angry swings			
poor decisions		risks safely avoided	/	rushed swings			
Penalties							
total		OB		lost		water	

Course				Yardage		Date	
Scoring							
gross		front 9		back 9		net	
eagles		birdies		pars		bogeys	
others		par 3's		par 4's		par 5's	
Greens in Regulation							
total	/ 18	7I - SW	/	1I - 6I	/	woods	/
Greens Under Regulation							
attempts		success		par 4's	/	par 5's	/
Shot-making							
wedges		short irons		mid-irons		long irons	
quality		quality		quality		quality	
fair		fair		fair		fair	
poor		poor		poor		poor	
Control							
wedges		short irons		mid-irons		long irons	
straight		straight		straight		straight	
left		left		left		left	
right		right		right		right	
Short Irons / Wedges Hit to Within:							
0' - 10'		10' - 30'		30' +		missed	
Fairways Hit							
total	/	driver	/	3W - 5W	/	irons	/
Driving							
quality		straight		solid		short	
fair		left		pulled		hooked	
poor		right		pushed		sliced	

Putting							
total		front 9		back 9		GIR	
1 putts		2 putts		3 putts		per GIR	
One Putts							
inside 5'	/	5' - 10'	/	10' - 20'	/	20' +	/
birdies	/	pars	/	bogeys	/	other	/
Missed Putts							
right		left		short		2' + long	
Long Putts Lagged to Within:							
tap-in		1' - 3'		3' - 5'		5' +	
Chipping							
holed		quality		fair		poor	
Pitching							
holed		quality		fair		poor	
chilly dip		pinched		skulled		fluffed	
Sand Play							
saves		0' - 5'		5' - 10'		10' +	
missed		left in		fat		skulled	
Mental Toughness							
bounce back	/	risks rewarded	/	lapses			
good decisions		risks punished	/	angry swings			
poor decisions		risks safely avoided	/	rushed swings			
Penalties							
total		OB		lost		water	

Course				Yardage		Date	
Scoring								
gross		front 9		back 9		net	
eagles		birdies		pars		bogeys	
others		par 3's		par 4's		par 5's	
Greens in Regulation								
total		/ 18	7I - SW	/	1I - 6I	/	woods	/
Greens Under Regulation								
attempts		success		par 4's	/	par 5's	/
Shot-making								
wedges		short irons		mid-irons		long irons	
quality		quality		quality		quality	
fair		fair		fair		fair	
poor		poor		poor		poor	
Control								
wedges		short irons		mid-irons		long irons	
straight		straight		straight		straight	
left		left		left		left	
right		right		right		right	
Short Irons / Wedges Hit to Within:								
0' - 10'		10' - 30'		30' +		missed	
Fairways Hit								
total		/	driver	/	3W - 5W	/	irons	/
Driving								
quality		straight		solid		short	
fair		left		pulled		hooked	
poor		right		pushed		sliced	

	Putting
total		front 9		back 9		GIR	
1 putts		2 putts		3 putts		per GIR	
	One Putts
inside 5'	/	5' - 10'	/	10' - 20'	/	20' +	/
birdies	/	pars	/	bogeys	/	other	/
	Missed Putts
right		left		short		2' + long	
	Long Putts Lagged to Within:
tap-in		1' - 3'		3' - 5'		5' +	
	Chipping
holed		quality		fair		poor	
	Pitching
holed		quality		fair		poor	
chilly dip		pinched		skulled		fluffed	
	Sand Play
saves		0' - 5'		5' - 10'		10' +	
missed		left in		fat		skulled	
	Mental Toughness
bounce back	/	risks rewarded	/	lapses			
good decisions		risks punished	/	angry swings			
poor decisions		risks safely avoided	/	rushed swings			
	Penalties
total		OB		lost		water	

Course				Yardage		Date	
Scoring							
gross		front 9		back 9		net	
eagles		birdies		pars		bogeys	
others		par 3's		par 4's		par 5's	
Greens in Regulation							
total	/ 18	7I - SW	/	1I - 6I	/	woods	/
Greens Under Regulation							
attempts		success		par 4's	/	par 5's	/
Shot-making							
wedges		short irons		mid-irons		long irons	
quality		quality		quality		quality	
fair		fair		fair		fair	
poor		poor		poor		poor	
Control							
wedges		short irons		mid-irons		long irons	
straight		straight		straight		straight	
left		left		left		left	
right		right		right		right	
Short Irons / Wedges Hit to Within:							
0' - 10'		10' - 30'		30' +		missed	
Fairways Hit							
total	/	driver	/	3W - 5W	/	irons	/
Driving							
quality		straight		solid		short	
fair		left		pulled		hooked	
poor		right		pushed		sliced	

	Putting						
total		front 9		back 9		GIR	
1 putts		2 putts		3 putts		per GIR	
	One Putts						
inside 5'	/	5' - 10'	/	10' - 20'	/	20' +	/
birdies	/	pars	/	bogeys	/	other	/
	Missed Putts						
right		left		short		2' + long	
	Long Putts Lagged to Within:						
tap-in		1' - 3'		3' - 5'		5' +	
	Chipping						
holed		quality		fair		poor	
	Pitching						
holed		quality		fair		poor	
chilly dip		pinched		skulled		fluffed	
	Sand Play						
saves		0' - 5'		5' - 10'		10' +	
missed		left in		fat		skulled	
	Mental Toughness						
bounce back	/	risks rewarded	/	lapses			
good decisions		risks punished	/	angry swings			
poor decisions		risks safely avoided	/	rushed swings			
	Penalties						
total		OB		lost		water	

Course			Yardage		Date	

Scoring

gross		front 9		back 9		net	
eagles		birdies		pars		bogeys	
others		par 3's		par 4's		par 5's	

Greens in Regulation

total		/ 18	7I - SW	/	1I - 6I	/	woods	/

Greens Under Regulation

attempts		success		par 4's	/	par 5's	/

Shot-making

wedges		short irons		mid-irons		long irons	
quality		quality		quality		quality	
fair		fair		fair		fair	
poor		poor		poor		poor	

Control

wedges		short irons		mid-irons		long irons	
straight		straight		straight		straight	
left		left		left		left	
right		right		right		right	

Short Irons / Wedges Hit to Within:

0' - 10'		10' - 30'		30' +		missed	

Fairways Hit

total		/	driver	/	3W - 5W	/	irons	/

Driving

quality		straight		solid		short	
fair		left		pulled		hooked	
poor		right		pushed		sliced	

Putting								
total		front 9		back 9		GIR	
1 putts		2 putts		3 putts		per GIR	
One Putts								
inside 5'		/	5' - 10'	/	10' - 20'	/	20' +	/
birdies		/	pars	/	bogeys	/	other	/
Missed Putts								
right		left		short		2' + long	
Long Putts Lagged to Within:								
tap-in		1' - 3'		3' - 5'		5' +	
Chipping								
holed		quality		fair		poor	
Pitching								
holed		quality		fair		poor	
chilly dip		pinched		skulled		fluffed	
Sand Play								
saves		0' - 5'		5' - 10'		10' +	
missed		left in		fat		skulled	
Mental Toughness								
bounce back		/	risks rewarded	/	lapses	
good decisions			risks punished	/	angry swings	
poor decisions			risks safely avoided	/	rushed swings	
Penalties								
total		OB		lost		water	

Course				Yardage		Date	
\multicolumn{8}{c}{Scoring}								
gross		front 9		back 9		net	
eagles		birdies		pars		bogeys	
others		par 3's		par 4's		par 5's	
\multicolumn{8}{c}{Greens in Regulation}								
total	/ 18	7I - SW	/	1I - 6I	/	woods	/
\multicolumn{8}{c}{Greens Under Regulation}								
attempts		success		par 4's	/	par 5's	/
\multicolumn{8}{c}{Shot-making}								
wedges		short irons		mid-irons		long irons	
quality		quality		quality		quality	
fair		fair		fair		fair	
poor		poor		poor		poor	
\multicolumn{8}{c}{Control}								
wedges		short irons		mid-irons		long irons	
straight		straight		straight		straight	
left		left		left		left	
right		right		right		right	
\multicolumn{8}{c}{Short Irons / Wedges Hit to Within:}								
0' - 10'		10' - 30'		30' +		missed	
\multicolumn{8}{c}{Fairways Hit}								
total	/	driver	/	3W - 5W	/	irons	/
\multicolumn{8}{c}{Driving}								
quality		straight		solid		short	
fair		left		pulled		hooked	
poor		right		pushed		sliced	

Putting								
total		front 9		back 9		GIR		
1 putts		2 putts		3 putts		per GIR		
One Putts								
inside 5'		/	5' - 10'	/	10' - 20'	/	20' +	/
birdies		/	pars	/	bogeys	/	other	/
Missed Putts								
right		left		short		2' + long		
Long Putts Lagged to Within:								
tap-in		1' - 3'		3' - 5'		5' +		
Chipping								
holed		quality		fair		poor		
Pitching								
holed		quality		fair		poor		
chilly dip		pinched		skulled		fluffed		
Sand Play								
saves		0' - 5'		5' - 10'		10' +		
missed		left in		fat		skulled		
Mental Toughness								
bounce back		/	risks rewarded	/	lapses			
good decisions			risks punished	/	angry swings			
poor decisions			risks safely avoided	/	rushed swings			
Penalties								
total		OB		lost		water		

The Golf Stats Log Book

71

Course				Yardage		Date	
Scoring							
gross		front 9		back 9		net	
eagles		birdies		pars		bogeys	
others		par 3's		par 4's		par 5's	
Greens in Regulation							
total	/ 18	7I - SW	/	1I - 6I	/	woods	/
Greens Under Regulation							
attempts		success		par 4's	/	par 5's	/
Shot-making							
wedges		short irons		mid-irons		long irons	
quality		quality		quality		quality	
fair		fair		fair		fair	
poor		poor		poor		poor	
Control							
wedges		short irons		mid-irons		long irons	
straight		straight		straight		straight	
left		left		left		left	
right		right		right		right	
Short Irons / Wedges Hit to Within:							
0' - 10'		10' - 30'		30' +		missed	
Fairways Hit							
total	/	driver	/	3W - 5W	/	irons	/
Driving							
quality		straight		solid		short	
fair		left		pulled		hooked	
poor		right		pushed		sliced	

\multicolumn{9}{c	}{Putting}
total		front 9		back 9		GIR	
1 putts		2 putts		3 putts		per GIR	
\multicolumn{9}{c	}{One Putts}
inside 5'		5' - 10'	/	10' - 20'	/	20' +	/
birdies	/	pars	/	bogeys	/	other	/
\multicolumn{9}{c	}{Missed Putts}
right		left		short		2' + long	
\multicolumn{9}{c	}{Long Putts Lagged to Within:}
tap-in		1' - 3'		3' - 5'		5' +	
\multicolumn{9}{c	}{Chipping}
holed		quality		fair		poor	
\multicolumn{9}{c	}{Pitching}
holed		quality		fair		poor	
chilly dip		pinched		skulled		fluffed	
\multicolumn{9}{c	}{Sand Play}
saves		0' - 5'		5' - 10'		10' +	
missed		left in		fat		skulled	
\multicolumn{9}{c	}{Mental Toughness}
bounce back	/	risks rewarded	/	lapses			
good decisions		risks punished	/	angry swings			
poor decisions		risks safely avoided	/	rushed swings			
\multicolumn{9}{c	}{Penalties}
total		OB		lost		water	

Course				Yardage		Date	
\multicolumn{8}{c}{Scoring}								
gross		front 9		back 9		net	
eagles		birdies		pars		bogeys	
others		par 3's		par 4's		par 5's	
\multicolumn{8}{c}{Greens in Regulation}								
total	/ 18	7I - SW	/	1I - 6I	/	woods	/
\multicolumn{8}{c}{Greens Under Regulation}								
attempts		success		par 4's	/	par 5's	/
\multicolumn{8}{c}{Shot-making}								
wedges		short irons		mid-irons		long irons	
quality		quality		quality		quality	
fair		fair		fair		fair	
poor		poor		poor		poor	
\multicolumn{8}{c}{Control}								
wedges		short irons		mid-irons		long irons	
straight		straight		straight		straight	
left		left		left		left	
right		right		right		right	
\multicolumn{8}{c}{Short Irons / Wedges Hit to Within:}								
0' - 10'		10' - 30'		30' +		missed	
\multicolumn{8}{c}{Fairways Hit}								
total	/	driver	/	3W - 5W	/	irons	/
\multicolumn{8}{c}{Driving}								
quality		straight		solid		short	
fair		left		pulled		hooked	
poor		right		pushed		sliced	

The Golf Stats Log Book

Putting						
total		front 9		back 9		GIR	
1 putts		2 putts		3 putts		per GIR	
One Putts						
inside 5'	/	5' - 10'	/	10' - 20'	/	20' +	/
birdies	/	pars	/	bogeys	/	other	/
Missed Putts						
right		left		short		2' + long	
Long Putts Lagged to Within:						
tap-in		1' - 3'		3' - 5'		5' +	
Chipping						
holed		quality		fair		poor	
Pitching						
holed		quality		fair		poor	
chilly dip		pinched		skulled		fluffed	
Sand Play						
saves		0' - 5'		5' - 10'		10' +	
missed		left in		fat		skulled	
Mental Toughness						
bounce back	/	risks rewarded	/	lapses	
good decisions		risks punished	/	angry swings	
poor decisions		risks safely avoided	/	rushed swings	
Penalties						
total		OB		lost		water	

Course				Yardage		Date	
\multicolumn{8}{c}{Scoring}							
gross		front 9		back 9		net	
eagles		birdies		pars		bogeys	
others		par 3's		par 4's		par 5's	
\multicolumn{8}{c}{Greens in Regulation}							
total	/ 18	7I - SW	/	1I - 6I	/	woods	/
\multicolumn{8}{c}{Greens Under Regulation}							
attempts		success		par 4's	/	par 5's	/
\multicolumn{8}{c}{Shot-making}							
wedges		short irons		mid-irons		long irons	
quality		quality		quality		quality	
fair		fair		fair		fair	
poor		poor		poor		poor	
\multicolumn{8}{c}{Control}							
wedges		short irons		mid-irons		long irons	
straight		straight		straight		straight	
left		left		left		left	
right		right		right		right	
\multicolumn{8}{c}{Short Irons / Wedges Hit to Within:}							
0' - 10'		10' - 30'		30' +		missed	
\multicolumn{8}{c}{Fairways Hit}							
total	/	driver	/	3W - 5W	/	irons	/
\multicolumn{8}{c}{Driving}							
quality		straight		solid		short	
fair		left		pulled		hooked	
poor		right		pushed		sliced	

Putting								
total		front 9		back 9		GIR		
1 putts		2 putts		3 putts		per GIR		
One Putts								
inside 5'		/	5' - 10'	/	10' - 20'	/	20' +	/
birdies		/	pars	/	bogeys	/	other	/
Missed Putts								
right		left		short		2' + long		
Long Putts Lagged to Within:								
tap-in		1' - 3'		3' - 5'		5' +		
Chipping								
holed		quality		fair		poor		
Pitching								
holed		quality		fair		poor		
chilly dip		pinched		skulled		fluffed		
Sand Play								
saves		0' - 5'		5' - 10'		10' +		
missed		left in		fat		skulled		
Mental Toughness								
bounce back		/	risks rewarded	/		lapses		
good decisions			risks punished	/		angry swings		
poor decisions			risks safely avoided	/		rushed swings		
Penalties								
total		OB		lost		water		

Course				Yardage		Date	
\multicolumn{8}{c}{Scoring}							
gross		front 9		back 9		net	
eagles		birdies		pars		bogeys	
others		par 3's		par 4's		par 5's	
\multicolumn{8}{c}{Greens in Regulation}							
total		/ 18	7I - SW	/	1I - 6I	/	woods	/
\multicolumn{8}{c}{Greens Under Regulation}							
attempts		success		par 4's	/	par 5's	/
\multicolumn{8}{c}{Shot-making}							
wedges		short irons		mid-irons		long irons	
quality		quality		quality		quality	
fair		fair		fair		fair	
poor		poor		poor		poor	
\multicolumn{8}{c}{Control}							
wedges		short irons		mid-irons		long irons	
straight		straight		straight		straight	
left		left		left		left	
right		right		right		right	
\multicolumn{8}{c}{Short Irons / Wedges Hit to Within:}							
0' - 10'		10' - 30'		30' +		missed	
\multicolumn{8}{c}{Fairways Hit}							
total		/	driver	/	3W - 5W	/	irons	/
\multicolumn{8}{c}{Driving}							
quality		straight		solid		short	
fair		left		pulled		hooked	
poor		right		pushed		sliced	

Putting							
total		front 9		back 9		GIR	
1 putts		2 putts		3 putts		per GIR	
One Putts							
inside 5'	/	5' - 10'	/	10' - 20'	/	20' +	/
birdies	/	pars	/	bogeys	/	other	/
Missed Putts							
right		left		short		2' + long	
Long Putts Lagged to Within:							
tap-in		1' - 3'		3' - 5'		5' +	
Chipping							
holed		quality		fair		poor	
Pitching							
holed		quality		fair		poor	
chilly dip		pinched		skulled		fluffed	
Sand Play							
saves		0' - 5'		5' - 10'		10' +	
missed		left in		fat		skulled	
Mental Toughness							
bounce back	/	risks rewarded	/	lapses			
good decisions		risks punished	/	angry swings			
poor decisions		risks safely avoided	/	rushed swings			
Penalties							
total		OB		lost		water	

The Golf Stats Log Book

Course				Yardage		Date	
\multicolumn{8}{c}{Scoring}							

Course				Yardage		Date	
gross		front 9		back 9		net	
eagles		birdies		pars		bogeys	
others		par 3's		par 4's		par 5's	

Scoring

gross		front 9		back 9		net	
eagles		birdies		pars		bogeys	
others		par 3's		par 4's		par 5's	

Greens in Regulation

total	/ 18	7I - SW	/	1I - 6I	/	woods	/

Greens Under Regulation

attempts		success		par 4's	/	par 5's	/

Shot-making

wedges		short irons		mid-irons		long irons	
quality		quality		quality		quality	
fair		fair		fair		fair	
poor		poor		poor		poor	

Control

wedges		short irons		mid-irons		long irons	
straight		straight		straight		straight	
left		left		left		left	
right		right		right		right	

Short Irons / Wedges Hit to Within:

0' - 10'		10' - 30'		30' +		missed	

Fairways Hit

total	/	driver	/	3W - 5W	/	irons	/

Driving

quality		straight		solid		short	
fair		left		pulled		hooked	
poor		right		pushed		sliced	

Putting							
total		front 9		back 9		GIR	
1 putts		2 putts		3 putts		per GIR	
One Putts							
inside 5'	/	5' - 10'	/	10' - 20'	/	20' +	/
birdies	/	pars	/	bogeys	/	other	/
Missed Putts							
right		left		short		2' + long	
Long Putts Lagged to Within:							
tap-in		1' - 3'		3' - 5'		5' +	
Chipping							
holed		quality		fair		poor	
Pitching							
holed		quality		fair		poor	
chilly dip		pinched		skulled		fluffed	
Sand Play							
saves		0' - 5'		5' - 10'		10' +	
missed		left in		fat		skulled	
Mental Toughness							
bounce back	/	risks rewarded	/	lapses			
good decisions		risks punished	/	angry swings			
poor decisions		risks safely avoided	/	rushed swings			
Penalties							
total		OB		lost		water	

Course				Yardage		Date	
Scoring							
gross		front 9		back 9		net	
eagles		birdies		pars		bogeys	
others		par 3's		par 4's		par 5's	
Greens in Regulation							
total	/ 18	7I - SW	/	1I - 6I	/	woods	/
Greens Under Regulation							
attempts		success		par 4's	/	par 5's	/
Shot-making							
wedges		short irons		mid-irons		long irons	
quality		quality		quality		quality	
fair		fair		fair		fair	
poor		poor		poor		poor	
Control							
wedges		short irons		mid-irons		long irons	
straight		straight		straight		straight	
left		left		left		left	
right		right		right		right	
Short Irons / Wedges Hit to Within:							
0' - 10'		10' - 30'		30' +		missed	
Fairways Hit							
total	/	driver	/	3W - 5W	/	irons	/
Driving							
quality		straight		solid		short	
fair		left		pulled		hooked	
poor		right		pushed		sliced	

Putting								
total		front 9		back 9		GIR	
1 putts		2 putts		3 putts		per GIR	
One Putts								
inside 5'	/	5' - 10'	/	10' - 20'	/	20' +	/
birdies	/	pars	/	bogeys	/	other	/
Missed Putts								
right		left		short		2' + long	
Long Putts Lagged to Within:								
tap-in		1' - 3'		3' - 5'		5' +	
Chipping								
holed		quality		fair		poor	
Pitching								
holed		quality		fair		poor	
chilly dip		pinched		skulled		fluffed	
Sand Play								
saves		0' - 5'		5' - 10'		10' +	
missed		left in		fat		skulled	
Mental Toughness								
bounce back	/	risks rewarded	/	lapses	
good decisions		risks punished	/	angry swings	
poor decisions		risks safely avoided	/	rushed swings	
Penalties								
total		OB		lost		water	

Course				Yardage		Date	
\multicolumn{8}{c}{Scoring}
gross		front 9		back 9		net	
eagles		birdies		pars		bogeys	
others		par 3's		par 4's		par 5's	
\multicolumn{8}{c}{Greens in Regulation}
total	/ 18	7I - SW	/	1I - 6I	/	woods	/
\multicolumn{8}{c}{Greens Under Regulation}
attempts		success		par 4's	/	par 5's	/
\multicolumn{8}{c}{Shot-making}
\multicolumn{2}{c}{wedges}	\multicolumn{2}{c}{short irons}	\multicolumn{2}{c}{mid-irons}	\multicolumn{2}{c}{long irons}
quality		quality		quality		quality	
fair		fair		fair		fair	
poor		poor		poor		poor	
\multicolumn{8}{c}{Control}
\multicolumn{2}{c}{wedges}	\multicolumn{2}{c}{short irons}	\multicolumn{2}{c}{mid-irons}	\multicolumn{2}{c}{long irons}
straight		straight		straight		straight	
left		left		left		left	
right		right		right		right	
\multicolumn{8}{c}{Short Irons / Wedges Hit to Within:}
0' - 10'		10' - 30'		30' +		missed	
\multicolumn{8}{c}{Fairways Hit}
total	/	driver	/	3W - 5W	/	irons	/
\multicolumn{8}{c}{Driving}
quality		straight		solid		short	
fair		left		pulled		hooked	
poor		right		pushed		sliced	

Putting								
total		front 9		back 9		GIR	
1 putts		2 putts		3 putts		per GIR	
One Putts								
inside 5'		/	5' - 10'	/	10' - 20'	/	20' +	/
birdies		/	pars	/	bogeys	/	other	/
Missed Putts								
right		left		short		2' + long	
Long Putts Lagged to Within:								
tap-in		1' - 3'		3' - 5'		5' +	
Chipping								
holed		quality		fair		poor	
Pitching								
holed		quality		fair		poor	
chilly dip		pinched		skulled		fluffed	
Sand Play								
saves		0' - 5'		5' - 10'		10' +	
missed		left in		fat		skulled	
Mental Toughness								
bounce back		/	risks rewarded	/		lapses	
good decisions			risks punished	/		angry swings	
poor decisions			risks safely avoided	/		rushed swings	
Penalties								
total		OB		lost		water	

Course			Yardage		Date	

Scoring						
gross		front 9		back 9		net	
eagles		birdies		pars		bogeys	
others		par 3's		par 4's		par 5's	

Greens in Regulation						
total		/ 18	7I - SW	/	1I - 6I	/	woods	/

Greens Under Regulation						
attempts		success		par 4's	/	par 5's	/

Shot-making						
wedges		short irons		mid-irons		long irons	
quality		quality		quality		quality	
fair		fair		fair		fair	
poor		poor		poor		poor	

Control						
wedges		short irons		mid-irons		long irons	
straight		straight		straight		straight	
left		left		left		left	
right		right		right		right	

Short Irons / Wedges Hit to Within:						
0' - 10'		10' - 30'		30' +		missed	

Fairways Hit						
total	/	driver	/	3W - 5W	/	irons	/

Driving						
quality		straight		solid		short	
fair		left		pulled		hooked	
poor		right		pushed		sliced	

Putting								
total		front 9		back 9		GIR	
1 putts		2 putts		3 putts		per GIR	
One Putts								
inside 5'	/	5' - 10'	/	10' - 20'	/	20' +	/
birdies	/	pars	/	bogeys	/	other	/
Missed Putts								
right		left		short		2' + long	
Long Putts Lagged to Within:								
tap-in		1' - 3'		3' - 5'		5' +	
Chipping								
holed		quality		fair		poor	
Pitching								
holed		quality		fair		poor	
chilly dip		pinched		skulled		fluffed	
Sand Play								
saves		0' - 5'		5' - 10'		10' +	
missed		left in		fat		skulled	
Mental Toughness								
bounce back	/	risks rewarded	/	lapses			
good decisions		risks punished	/	angry swings			
poor decisions		risks safely avoided	/	rushed swings			
Penalties								
total		OB		lost		water	

Course				Yardage		Date	
\multicolumn{8}{c}{Scoring}							

Course				Yardage		Date	
gross		front 9		back 9		net	
eagles		birdies		pars		bogeys	
others		par 3's		par 4's		par 5's	

Scoring

gross		front 9		back 9		net	
eagles		birdies		pars		bogeys	
others		par 3's		par 4's		par 5's	

Greens in Regulation

total	/ 18	7I - SW	/	1I - 6I	/	woods	/

Greens Under Regulation

attempts		success		par 4's	/	par 5's	/

Shot-making

wedges		short irons		mid-irons		long irons	
quality		quality		quality		quality	
fair		fair		fair		fair	
poor		poor		poor		poor	

Control

wedges		short irons		mid-irons		long irons	
straight		straight		straight		straight	
left		left		left		left	
right		right		right		right	

Short Irons / Wedges Hit to Within:

0' - 10'		10' - 30'		30' +		missed	

Fairways Hit

total	/	driver	/	3W - 5W	/	irons	/

Driving

quality		straight		solid		short	
fair		left		pulled		hooked	
poor		right		pushed		sliced	

Putting							
total		front 9		back 9		GIR	
1 putts		2 putts		3 putts		per GIR	
One Putts							
inside 5'	/	5' - 10'	/	10' - 20'	/	20' +	/
birdies	/	pars	/	bogeys	/	other	/
Missed Putts							
right		left		short		2' + long	
Long Putts Lagged to Within:							
tap-in		1' - 3'		3' - 5'		5' +	
Chipping							
holed		quality		fair		poor	
Pitching							
holed		quality		fair		poor	
chilly dip		pinched		skulled		fluffed	
Sand Play							
saves		0' - 5'		5' - 10'		10' +	
missed		left in		fat		skulled	
Mental Toughness							
bounce back	/	risks rewarded	/	lapses			
good decisions		risks punished	/	angry swings			
poor decisions		risks safely avoided	/	rushed swings			
Penalties							
total		OB		lost		water	

The Golf Stats Log Book

Course				Yardage		Date	
Scoring								
gross		front 9		back 9		net	
eagles		birdies		pars		bogeys	
others		par 3's		par 4's		par 5's	
Greens in Regulation								
total	/ 18	7I - SW	/	1I - 6I	/	woods	/
Greens Under Regulation								
attempts		success		par 4's	/	par 5's	/
Shot-making								
wedges		short irons		mid-irons		long irons	
quality		quality		quality		quality	
fair		fair		fair		fair	
poor		poor		poor		poor	
Control								
wedges		short irons		mid-irons		long irons	
straight		straight		straight		straight	
left		left		left		left	
right		right		right		right	
Short Irons / Wedges Hit to Within:								
0' - 10'		10' - 30'		30' +		missed	
Fairways Hit								
total	/	driver	/	3W - 5W	/	irons	/
Driving								
quality		straight		solid		short	
fair		left		pulled		hooked	
poor		right		pushed		sliced	

Putting								
total		front 9		back 9		GIR	
1 putts		2 putts		3 putts		per GIR	
One Putts								
inside 5'		/	5' - 10'	/	10' - 20'	/	20' +	/
birdies		/	pars	/	bogeys	/	other	/
Missed Putts								
right		left		short		2' + long	
Long Putts Lagged to Within:								
tap-in		1' - 3'		3' - 5'		5' +	
Chipping								
holed		quality		fair		poor	
Pitching								
holed		quality		fair		poor	
chilly dip		pinched		skulled		fluffed	
Sand Play								
saves		0' - 5'		5' - 10'		10' +	
missed		left in		fat		skulled	
Mental Toughness								
bounce back		/	risks rewarded	/	lapses		
good decisions			risks punished	/	angry swings		
poor decisions			risks safely avoided	/	rushed swings		
Penalties								
total		OB		lost		water	

Course				Yardage		Date	
Scoring							
gross		front 9		back 9		net	
eagles		birdies		pars		bogeys	
others		par 3's		par 4's		par 5's	
Greens in Regulation							
total	/ 18	7I - SW	/	1I - 6I	/	woods	/
Greens Under Regulation							
attempts		success		par 4's	/	par 5's	/
Shot-making							
wedges		short irons		mid-irons		long irons	
quality		quality		quality		quality	
fair		fair		fair		fair	
poor		poor		poor		poor	
Control							
wedges		short irons		mid-irons		long irons	
straight		straight		straight		straight	
left		left		left		left	
right		right		right		right	
Short Irons / Wedges Hit to Within:							
0' - 10'		10' - 30'		30' +		missed	
Fairways Hit							
total	/	driver	/	3W - 5W	/	irons	/
Driving							
quality		straight		solid		short	
fair		left		pulled		hooked	
poor		right		pushed		sliced	

Putting								
total		front 9		back 9		GIR		
1 putts		2 putts		3 putts		per GIR		
One Putts								
inside 5'	/	5' - 10'	/	10' - 20'	/	20' +	/	
birdies	/	pars	/	bogeys	/	other	/	
Missed Putts								
right		left		short		2' + long		
Long Putts Lagged to Within:								
tap-in		1' - 3'		3' - 5'		5' +		
Chipping								
holed		quality		fair		poor		
Pitching								
holed		quality		fair		poor		
chilly dip		pinched		skulled		fluffed		
Sand Play								
saves		0' - 5'		5' - 10'		10' +		
missed		left in		fat		skulled		
Mental Toughness								
bounce back	/	risks rewarded	/	lapses				
good decisions		risks punished	/	angry swings				
poor decisions		risks safely avoided	/	rushed swings				
Penalties								
total		OB		lost		water		

CPSIA information can be obtained at www.ICGtesting.com
Printed in the USA
LVOW03s1907120115

422514LV00021B/1292/P